Supreme Court of Illinois et al., Petitioners,
v. Basil D. Ktsanes. U.S. Supreme Court
Transcript of Record with Supporting Pleadings

HERBERT LEE CAPLAN, JASON E BELLOWS

Supreme Court of Illinois et al., Petitioners, v. Basil D. Ktsanes.

Petition / HERBERT LEE CAPLAN / 1977 / 77-691 / 435 U.S. 933 / 98 S.Ct. 1508 / 55 L.Ed.2d 530 / 11-11-1977
Supreme Court of Illinois et al., Petitioners, v. Basil D. Ktsanes.
Brief in Opposition (P) / JASON E BELLOWS / 1977 / 77-691 / 435 U.S. 933 / 98 S.Ct. 1508 / 55 L.Ed.2d 530 / 2-14-1978

Supreme Court of Illinois et al., Petitioners, v.
Basil D. Ktsanes. U.S. Supreme Court Transcript
of Record with Supporting Pleadings

Table of Contents

IN THE

Supreme Court of the United States

OCTOBER TERM, 1977

No. 77-691

77-691

SUPREME COURT OF ILLINOIS, HON. DANIEL P. WARD, HON. ROBERT C. UNDERWOOD, HON. JOSEPH H. GOLDENHERSH, HON. HOWARD C. RYAN, HON. WILLIAM G. CLARK, HON. THOMAS J. MORAN, HON. JAMES A. DOOLEY, JUSTICES OF THE SUPREME COURT OF ILLINOIS; LEN Y. SMITH, CLYDE O. BOWLES, JR., JOHN B. HENDRICKS, GEORGE B. LEE, AND FRANCIS D. MORRISSEY, MEMBERS OF THE STATE BOARD OF LAW EXAMINERS,

Petitioners,

VS.

BASIL D. KTSANES,

Respondent.

PETITION FOR WRIT OF CERTIORARI TO THE UNITED STATES COURT OF APPEALS FOR THE SEVENTH CIRCUIT

WILLIAM J. SCOTT,
Attorney General of Illinois,
160 N. LaSalle Street,
Chicago, Illinois 60601,
Attorney for Petitioners.

HERBERT LEE CAPLAN,
Assistant Attorney General,
(312) 793-3813
Of Counsel.

Keener Printing Company ——— 265

INDEX

TABLE OF AUTHORITIES

Federal Cases

Supreme Court of the United States

OCTOBER TERM, 1977

No.

SUPREME COURT OF ILLINOIS, HON. DANIEL P.
WARD, HON. ROBERT C. UNDERWOOD, HON.
JOSEPH H. GOLDENHERSH, HON. HOWARD C.
RYAN, HON. WILLIAM G. CLARK, HON. THOMAS
J. MORAN, HON. JAMES A. DOOLEY, JUSTICES
OF THE SUPREME COURT OF ILLINOIS; LEN Y.
SMITH, CLYDE O. BOWLES, JR., JOHN B. HEND-
RICKS, GEORGE B. LEE, AND FRANCIS D. MOR-
RISSEY, MEMBERS OF THE STATE BOARD OF
LAW EXAMINERS,

Petitioners,

vs.

BASIL D. KTSANES,

Respondent.

PETITION FOR WRIT OF CERTIORARI TO THE UNITED STATES COURT OF APPEALS FOR THE SEVENTH CIRCUIT

Petitioners, Supreme Court of Illinois, Hon. Daniel P. Ward, Hon. Robert C. Underwood, Hon. Joseph H. Goldenhersh, Hon. Howard C. Ryan, Hon. William G. Clark, Hon. Thomas J. Moran, Hon. James A. Dooley, Justices of the Supreme Court of Illinois; Len Y. Smith, Clyde O. Bowles, Jr., John B. Hendricks, George B. Lee, and Francis Morrissey, members of the State Board of Law Examiners, respectfully pray that a Writ of Certiorari issue to review the judgment and opinion of the United States Court of Appeals for the Seventh Circuit entered in this proceeding on March 23, 1977, as supplemented on August 15, 1977 on denial of petition for rehearing.

OPINION BELOW

The opinion of the United States Court of Appeals for the Seventh Circuit is reported at 552 F. 2d 740 and is included herein as Appendix A. The supplemental opinion on denial of petition for rehearing is reported at 560 F. 2d 790 and is included herein as Appendix B. The opinion of the district court is not reported and is included herein as Appendix C.

JURISDICTION

The judgment of the Court of Appeals was entered on March 23, 1977. A timely petition for rehearing and suggestion of rehearing en banc was denied on August 15, 1977. This Court's jurisdiction is invoked under 28 U.S.C. § 1254(1), 2101(c) and 2106.

QUESTION PRESENTED

Whether a decision of the Illinois Supreme Court denying an applicant admission to practice without examination on foreign license may be reviewed and collaterally attacked by an original action in federal district court.

CONSTITUTION AND REGULATION INVOLVED

Tenth Amendment to Constitution of the United States:

> "The powers not delegated to the United States by the Constitution nor prohibited by it to the States, are reserved to the States respectively, or to the people."

Eleventh Amendment to Constitution of the United States:

> "The judicial power of the United States shall not be construed to extend to any suit in law or equity, commenced or prosecuted against one of the United States by Citizens of another State, or by Citizens or Subjects of any Foreign State."

Rule 705(d) Illinois Supreme Court.

Ill. Rev. Stats., 1975, Chap. 110A, § 705(d):

> "(d) An applicant who has taken and failed to pass the bar examination in Illinois shall not be eligible to apply for admission on foreign license."

STATEMENT OF THE CASE

This is an action brought pursuant to 42 U.S.C. § 1983 against the Justices of the Illinois Supreme Court and the court-appointed members of the State Board of Law Examiners, to enjoin enforcement of Illinois Supreme Court Rule 705(d) and overturn a final decision of the court which denied respondent's petition to be admitted to the bar of Illinois without the requirement that he successfully pass the Illinois written bar examination.

The complaint alleges that respondent had failed the Illinois written bar examination but was subsequently admitted to the bar of Kentucky and is entitled to be admitted to practice in Illinois as a foreign licensee.

The Illinois Supreme Court is the highest court of the State of Illinois [Ill. Const. Art. VI, § 4] and, inter alia, prescribes general qualifications for admission to practice law in Illinois [Sup. Ct. Rule 701(a), 705(d)] and appoints a Board of Law Examiners to conduct written bar examinations. [Sup. Ct. Rule 702, 704]

Respondent has taken and failed to pass the Illinois written bar examination. An unsuccessful applicant may take successive written examinations until he is able to qualify. [Sup. Ct. 704(d)]

Respondent did not retake the Illinois written bar examination but, instead, moved to Kentucky and approximately one year later was admitted to the Kentucky bar. Respondent subsequently returned to the State of Illinois and sought admission to the Illinois Bar upon foreign license without the requirement that he successfully pass the Illinois written bar examination.

Illinois Supreme Court Rule 705(d) expressly provides:

"An applicant who has taken and failed to pass the bar examination in Illinois shall not be eligible to apply for admission on foreign license." [Ill. Rev. Stats. 1975, chap. 110A, § 705(d)]

The State Board of Law Examiners informed respondent of the existence of Supreme Court Rule 705 (d) and its application to his case. Respondent petitioned the Illinois Supreme Court for admission to practice and waiver of the rule in his case. On March 18, 1975, the Illinois Supreme Court denied respondent's petition for waiver of Rule 705(d) and for admission to the bar of Illinois without examination on foreign license.

Respondent did not seek review of the adverse Illinois Supreme Court decision before the United States Supreme Court.

Approximately seven months after denial of his state court petition, respondent filed suit in the United States District Court for the Northern District of Illinois, Eastern Division, seeking to enjoin the Illinois Supreme Court and the Board of Law Examiners from enforcing Rule 705(d) against him and to declare the rule to be in violation of the Equal Protection Clause of the Fourteenth Amendment to the United States Constitution.

Petitioners filed a motion to dismiss the complaint pursuant to Rule 12(b)(1),(2),(6), Fed. R. Civ. P. On April 20, 1976, the Honorable Joseph Sam Perry entered an order dismissing the complaint for lack of district court jurisdiction and failure to present a substantial federal question. [App. C]

An appeal was then taken to the United States Court of Appeals for the Seventh Circuit, which on March 23, 1977, reversed the decision of the district court [App. A], concluding that:

"[petitioners'] denial of [respondent's] request for an exemption from Rule 705(d) of the Supreme Court of Illinois was purely an administrative act and did not qualify as a 'case or controversy' under Article III of the Constitution so as to render it directly appealable to the Supreme Court of the United States. Thus, there existed no jurisdictional bar under the doctrines of *res judicata* or collateral estoppel to federal consideration of [respondent's] constitutional claims because [respondent's] action was not a collateral attack upon a *judicial* decision rendered by the Illinois Supreme Court." (Emphasis in original.)

Petition for rehearing and suggestion of rehearing *en banc* was denied on August 15, 1977. [App. B]

REASONS FOR GRANTING THE WRIT

I.

THE DECISION OF THE SEVENTH CIRCUIT IS IN CONFLICT WITH DECISIONS OF OTHER COURTS OF APPEALS AND APPLICABLE DECISIONS OF THE SUPREME COURT.

The opinion of the Seventh Circuit Court of Appeals entered March 23, 1977, as supplemented on August 15, 1977, holds, apparently for the first time, that a denial by the Illinois Supreme Court of a petition for admission to the bar may be collaterally attacked and relitigated by a de novo action in the district court. Petitioners contend that the district court lacks subject matter jurisdiction.

The operative facts of the case are not in dispute. Plaintiff filed a "Petition for Admission to the Bar of Illinois" before the Illinois Supreme Court seeking admission without examination, notwithstanding Supreme Court Rule 705(d).* The petition was denied on March 18, 1975. No

---

*Reference to "a reciprocity agreement" in the circuit court's opinion is incorrect. (App. A4) Admission is based solely upon the practice requirement detailed in Rule 705 and not upon reciprocity.

appeal was taken. Seven months later the instant action was filed in the district court challenging the denial of admission to the bar on federal constitutional grounds.

The allegations in the district court complaint are identical to the allegations in the Supreme Court petition, except for the additional legal argument that the Supreme Court policy expressed in Rule 705(d) "has no rational connection with the plaintiff's fitness or capacity to practice law," and "is contrary to the Equal Protection Clause of the Fourteenth Amendment to the Constitution of the United States."

In *In Re Summers*, 325 U.S. 561, 65 S. Ct. 1307 (1945), the United States Supreme Court held that the denial of a petition for admission to the practice of law by the Illinois Supreme Court is a case or controversy or judicial proceeding that is directly reviewable by the United States Supreme Court. The Court held:

> "A claim of a present right to admission to the bar of a state and denial of that right is a controversy. When the claim is made in a state court and a denial of that right is made by judicial order, it is a case which may be reviewed under Article III of the Constitution when federal questions are raised and proper steps taken to that end, in this Court." 325 U.S. at 568-569.

Title 28 U.S.C.§ 1257 provides that:

> "Final judgments or decrees rendered by the highest court of a State in which a decision could be had. may be reviewed by the Supreme Court. . . ."

Title 28 U.S.C.§ 2104 provides that: '
> "An appeal to the Supreme Court from a State court shall be taken in the same manner and under the same regulations, and shall have the same effect, as if the judgment or decree appealed from had been rendered in a court of the United States."

In *Doe* v. *Pringle,* 550 F. 2d 596 (10th Cir. 1976), cert. den., ——U.S.——, 97 S. Ct. 2179 (1977), the plaintiff was denied bar admission by the Colorado Supreme Court because he had been convicted of a felony. As in the case at bar, he petitioned the Supreme Court for admission, contending he had been rehabilitated and was presently fit to practice. The petition was denied. No appeal was taken, and a de novo action was filed in the district court under Section 1983 alleging that the Colorado Supreme Court had acted arbitrarily and capriciously and had denied him equal protection of the law. The Tenth Circuit held that the district court:

> "is without subject matter jurisdiction to review a final order of the Colorado Supreme Court denying *a particular application for admission* to the Colorado Bar. This rule applies even though, as here, the challenge is anchored to alleged deprivations of federally protected due process and equal protection rights." (Emphasis added in original.)

The applicable and controlling principles of law, as they apply in the case at bar as well, were succinctly summarized in the concurring opinion of Judge Breitenstein:

> "Doe's sole claim is that in his particular situation the actions of the Colorado Supreme Court denied his federal constitutional rights to due process and equal protection. The action of the Colorado court was judicial rather than administrative. A federal district court does not sit as an appellate court to review actions of a State Supreme Court. Doe's recourse was to petition the Supreme Court of the United States for certiorari review of the action of the state supreme court."

In *MacKay* v. *Nesbitt,* 412 F. 2d 846 (9th Cir. 1969), the plaintiff filed an action in the district court seeking to have a disciplinary order of the Alaska Supreme Court enjoined and declared void. Suit was dismissed for want of jurisdiction and the Ninth Circuit affirmed, saying:

"Language in *Theard v. United States*, 354 U.S. 278, 281, 77 S. Ct. 1274, 1 L. Ed. 2d 1342 (1957). and holdings in *Gately v. Sutton*, 310 F. 2d 107, 108 (10th Cir. 1962); *Jones v. Hulse*, 391 F. 2d 198, 202 (8th Cir. 1968); and *Lenske v. Sercombe*, 266 F. Supp. 609, 612 (D. Ore. 1967). support the *rule that orders of a state court relating to the admission, discipline, and disbarment of members of its bar may be reviewed only by the Supreme Court of the United States on certiorari to the State court, and not by means of an original action in a lower federal court.* The rule serves substantial policy interests arising from the historic relationship between the state and federal judicial systems. We are persuaded that it is sound." 412 F. 2d at 846. (Emphasis added.)

In *Jones v. Hulse*. 391 F. 2d 198 (8th Cir. 1968), an action was filed in the United States District Court to enjoin the enforcement of a Missouri Supreme Court mandate suspending an attorney's license to practice law. The District Court dismissed for lack of jurisdiction and the Court of Appeals affirmed. In reaching its decision, the Eighth Circuit said:

"Irrespective of how appellant labels his lawsuit, we are convinced that his action is tantamount to an appeal or a petition to review the propriety of the state court order.

The pronouncement of the Supreme Court in *Rooker v. Fidelity Trust Company*, 263 U.S. 413, 44 S. Ct. 149, 68 L. Ed. 362 (1923), is apropos here:

'If the constitutional questions stated in the * * * [complaint] actually arose in the cause, it was the province and duty of the state courts to decide them; and their decision. whether right or wrong, was an exercise of jurisdiction. If the decision was wrong, that did not make the judgment void, but merely left it open to reversal or modification in an appropriate and timely appellate proceeding. Unless and until so reversed or modified, it would be an effective and conclusive adjudication. [Citation omitted.] Under the legislation of Congress, no court of the United States other than this Court could entertain a proceeding to reverse or modify the judgment for errors of that character. * * * To do so would be an exercise of appellate jurisdiction. The jurisdiction possessed by the District Courts is strictly original.' 263 U.S. at 415-416, 44 S. Ct. at 150.

* * *

All we are required to decide is whether on this record appellant is entitled to invoke the original jurisdiction of the federal courts for the purpose of obtaining an adjudication as to the validity of the judgment of the Missouri Court. We are fully convinced that no grounds exist for federal jurisdiction and that the order of dismissal was proper." 391 F. 2d at 202.

Mr. Justice Frankfurter, in his concurring opinion in *Schware* v. *Board of Bar Examiners of the State of New Mexico*, 353 U.S. 232, 77 S. Ct. 752 (1957), articulated the policy considerations underlying federal jurisdiction to review state court orders relating to admission to the practice of law:

"Admission to practice in a State and before its courts necessarily belongs to that State. Of course, legislation laying down general conditions of an arbitrary or discriminatory character may, like other legislation, fall afoul of the Fourteenth Amendment. . . . A very different question is presented when this Court is asked to review the exercise of judgment in refusing admission to the bar in an individual case, such as we have here.

It is beyond this Court's function to act as overseer of a particular result of the procedure established by a particular State for admission to its bar." 353 U.S. at 248.

Respondent herein seeks the same result in both the Illinois Supreme Court and District Court, to-wit, his own admission to practice without examination. It is the denial of that admission that he continues to litigate by an original action in the district court. Respondent has brought suit individually and not as a class representative. The complaint does not purport to be a class action and respondent has made no effort to comply with Rule 23, Fed. R. Civ. P. It is clear that plaintiff attacks Supreme Court Rule 705(d) only as applied to the facts in his own case by the Illinois Supreme Court.

Most recently, in *Richardson et al. v. McFadden et al.*, No. 73-2512. ——F. 2d—— (4th Cir., Oct. 12, 1977), copy of which is attached hereto as Appendix D, involving the efforts of individual applicants to achieve bar admission, the concurring opinions of the Fourth Circuit review the applicable case decisions throughout the country and similarly reach a conclusion which is contrary to the Seventh Circuit:

> "Settled precedents, I believe, support my views regarding the district court's lack of subject matter jurisdiction." (App. D5)

Thus, the judgment and opinion of the Seventh Circuit finding subject matter jurisdiction to exist in the district court is in conflict with the decisions of other courts of appeal and applicable decisions of the Supreme Court.

II.

SOUND PRINCIPLES OF "EQUITY, AMITY AND FEDERALISM" PRECLUDE AN EXERCISE OF ORIGINAL JURISDICTION BY THE DISTRICT COURT.

The legal posture of the case at bar is remarkably similar to *Juidice v. Vail*, 430 U.S.——, 97 S. Ct. 1211, 1214, 1218 (March 22, 1977). In *Juidice*, after State civil collection proceedings, a judgment debtor filed suit in the district court raising for the first time Fourteenth Amendment arguments to challenge the State law.

In reversing a three judge district court which had certified a class, declared the State statute unconstitutional and permanently enjoined its enforcement, the United States Supreme Court held:

> "As they never appeared in the New York courts, *they obviously did not raise these constitutional claims in the state court proceedings. The contentions made before the District Court, however, could have been raised by appellees in the state courts,* as a defense to the ongoing proceedings. *Had the county court ruled against these contentions, appellees could have appealed them to the Appellate Term of the Supreme Court. They chose, by resorting to the federal courts, not to avail themselves of this forum afforded them by the State of New York. We must decide whether, with the existence of an available forum for raising constitutional issues in a state judicial proceeding, the United States District Court could properly entertain appellees'* § 1983 *action* in light of our decisions in *Younger* v. *Harris,* 401 U.S. 37, 91 S. Ct. 746, 27 L. Ed. 2d 669 (1971), and *Huffman* v. *Pursue, Ltd.,* 420 U.S. 592, 95 S. Ct. 1200, 43 L. Ed. 2d 482 (1975). We hold that it could not.

> *   *   *

> We now hold, however, that the principles of *Younger* and *Huffman* are not confined solely to the types of state actions which were sought to be enjoined in those cases. As we emphasized in *Huffman,* the 'more vital consideration' behind the *Younger* doctrine of nonintervention lay not in the fact that the state criminal process was involved, but rather in

>> 'the notion of "comity," that is, a proper respect for state functions, a recognition of the fact that the entire country is made up of a Union of separate state governments, and a continuance of the

belief that the National Government will fare best if the States and their institutions are left free to perform their separate functions in their separate ways.' *Huffman, supra,* at 601, 95 S. Ct., at 1206, quoting *Younger, supra,* 401 U.S. at 44, 91 S. Ct. at 750.

* * *

Here it is abundantly clear that appellees had an opportunity to present their federal claims in the State proceedinug. No more is required to invoke *Younger* abstention." (Emphasis added.)

Neither respondent nor the Seventh Circuit opinion deny that constitutional claims could have been raised and adjudicated in the proceedings before the Illinois Supreme Court. Admittedly, respondent has had one bite at the apple. He now seeks to relitigate his afterthoughts by a second action in a fresh forum, and thus to collaterally review and overturn the order of the State court which denied him admission to the bar without examination.[e] The well established rule against such bifurcated proceedings has added compulsion when considerations of "equity, comity, and federalism" coexist as they do in matters of bar admission.

CONCLUSION

Respondent originally petitioned the Illinois Supreme Court to be admitted to the Illinois Bar upon foreign license and without the requirement that he satisfactorily pass a written bar examination.

The state court petition of respondent was denied by the Illinois Supreme Court.

---

[e]Plaintiff still is not precluded from retaking the Illinois bar examination to demonstrate qualification for admission, as provided in Rule 704.

Respondent failed to seek or perfect review of the decision of the Illinois Supreme Court in the United States Supreme Court.

Respondent has attempted to collaterally attack and overturn the decision of the Illinois Supreme Court by an original action in the federal district court.

The district court lacks subject matter jurisdiction.

The decision of the Seventh Circuit Court of Appeals reversing dismissal by the district court is in conflict with the decisions of other courts of appeals and applicable decisions of the United States Supreme Court on the same matter.

WHEREFORE, Petitioners pray that a writ of certiorari issue to review the judgment and opinion of the United States Court of Appeals for the Seventh Circuit entered on March 23, 1977 as supplemented on August 15, 1977.

Respectfully submitted,

WILLIAM J. SCOTT,
Attorney General of Illinois,
160 N. LaSalle Street,
Chicago, Illinois 60601,

Attorney for Petitioners.

HERBERT LEE CAPLAN,
Assistant Attorney General,
(312) 793-3813
Of Counsel.

No. 76-1623

BASIL D. KTSANES,

Plaintiff-Appellant,

vs.

HONORABLE ROBERT C. UNDERWOOD, et al.,

Defendants-Appellees.

Apeal from the United States District Court
for the Northern District of Illinois,
Eastern Division.
No. 75 C 3421
Joseph Sam Perry, *Judge.*

Argued December 2, 1976 — Decided March 23, 1977

Before FAIRCHILD, *Chief Judge,* HASTINGS, *Senior Circuit Judge,*[1] and SWYGERT, *Circuit Judge.*

SWYGERT, *Circuit Judge.* Rule 705 of the Illinois Supreme Court (Smith-Hurd Ill. Ann. Stats. Ch. 110A § 705) provides that an attorney who has resided and practiced law in another state for five years may, upon passing a character and fitness test, be admitted to the

---

1. Senior Circuit Judge John S. Hastings heard oral argument and participated in the conference of the court, but died before this opinion was submitted to him for approval.

bar of Illinois.[2] The rule further provides that an otherwise qualified attorney who has practiced in another state

---

2. Illinois Supreme Court Rule 705 provides in part:

(a) Any person who has been admitted to practice in the highest court of law in any other State or territory of the United States or the District of Columbia, or admitted to practice as an attorney (or the equivalent) in another country whose jurisprudence is based upon the principles of the English common law, may make application to the Board of Law Examiners for admission to the bar without examination upon the following conditions:

(1) The educational qualifications of the applicant are such as would entitle him to write the bar examination in this State at the time he seeks admission; and he has resided and actively and continuously practiced law in such other jurisdiction for at least three years within the period of five years immediately prior to making application in Illinois.

(2) Any person who is unable to meet the requirements set forth above in (1) may be admitted to the bar of Illinois without examination if he has actively and continuously practiced law in such other jurisdiction for a period of at least five years within the period of seven years immediately prior to making application in Illinois.

* * *

(c) In the event the Board of Law Examiners shall find that such aplicant meets the requirements of this rule and has received from the Committee on Character and Fitness its certification of good moral character and general fitness to practice law, the board shall certify to the court that such applicant is qualified for admission.

is ineligible to apply for admission if that attorney has previously taken and failed an Illinois bar examination.[3]

This appeal presents two issues: (1) whether the Illinois Supreme Court's denial of plaintiff-appellant's petition for waiver of Rule 705(d) and admission to the bar of Illinois on foreign license is a judicial proceeding directly reviewable by the United States Supreme Court, thus rendering the district court without jurisdiction to consider an attack on that denial; and if not, (2) whether the plaintiff-appellant presented a substantial federal question requiring the convening of a three-judge court. We hold that the petition for waiver of Rule 705(d) and its denial did not constitute a judicial proceeding appealable to the United States Supreme Court. We further hold that a substantial federal question exists which requires the consideration of a three-judge court.[4]

Plaintiff Basil D. Ktsanes brought this action against the Justices of the Illinois Supreme Court and the members of the State Board of Law Examiners pursuant to 42 U.S.C. § 1983. Plaintiff requested the convening of a three-judge court under 28 U.S.C. § 2281 for a declaration that Rule 705(d) of the Supreme Court of Illinois is void and unenforceable, and for an injunction against enforcement

---

3. Rule 705(d) provides:

An applicant who has taken and failed to pass the bar examination in Illinois shall not be eligible to apply for admission on foreign license.

4. Because this action in the district court was commenced before August 12, 1976, the applicability of 28 U.S.C. § 2281 is not affected by the repeal of that statute by Pub. L. No. 94-381 [S. 537]; August 12, 1976; 90 Stat. 1119.

of the rule by defendants. The plaintiff alleged that Rule 705(d) violates the Equal Protection Clause of the Fourteenth Amendment.

The district court granted deefndants' motion to dismiss, refusing to convene a three-judge court. This appeal followed.

Plaintiff was born in Illinois and resided there until he went to Louisville, Kentucky to attend law school. He graduated in June 1967 and returned to Illinois where he took the Illinois bar examination in July and failed to pass. When he could not find satisfactory employment in Illinois, plaintiff returned to Louisville where he found a position with the Jefferson County Attorney's office.

In July 1968 the plaintiff passed the Kentucky bar examination and was appointed as assistant county attorney. In April 1969 he accepted a position as legal assistant to the Governor of Kentucky in the Department of Finance, and in August 1970 was promoted to deputy finance commissioner. He also served as an assistant commonwealth attorney.

A reciprocity agreement permitting admission on foreign license exists between Illinois and Kentucky. Plaintiff requested an application from the Illinois State Board of Law Examiners; it was denied under Rule 705(d) because he had previously failed the Illinois bar examination. He then petitioned the Justices of the Illinois Supreme Court for an exemption from the rule. The petition was denied in March 1975. Ktsanes subsequently filed this action in federal court under section 1983.

The threshold issue is whether there was jurisdiction to hear a constitutional challenge to Rule 705(d) in the district court. If jurisdiction exists, we must decide whether the issues present a substantial federal question, necessary in order to convene a three-judge court.

I

The Attorney General of the State of Illinois on behalf of the defendants argue that there is no jurisdiction to hear this case because it amounts to a review of a decision of the Illinois Supreme Court by a federal district court. Proper procedure, he contends, would have been an appeal from the Illinois court directly to the Supreme Court of the United States under 28 U.S.C. § 1257. We do not agree.

The United States Supreme Court in a previous challenge to the right of the Illinois Supreme Court to exclude a person from the bar of that state considered the requirement of a case or controversy under Article III of the federal Constitution. *In re Summers*, 325 U.S. 561 (1945). In that case the plaintiff, a conscientious objector, had been excluded from the bar because he would not take the required oath to support the constitution of Illinois. He alleged that the exclusion was in violation of the Due Process clause of the Fourteenth Amendment based upon First Amendment freedom of religion grounds. Summers had completed all the prerequisites for admission to the bar except that the committee on character and fitness had not certified him. He filed a petition for admission in the Illinois Supreme Court, alleging that he had been refused the certificate because he was a conscientious objector and that this was in violation of the Fourteenth Amendment. The petition was denied. In the United States Supreme Court, the defendants, the Justices of the Illinois Supreme Court, argued that the constitutional issue raised could not be considered because there was no case or controversy and the Supreme Court, therefore, lacked jurisdiction. The Court held, however, that a true controversy did exist. The standard used in this determination is necessarily a federal one arising from the requirement in Article III, § 2, Cl. 1 of the Constitution.[5] *In re Summers, supra* at 566; *Nashville, C. & St. L. Ry. Co.* v. *Wallace,* 288 U.S. 249, 259 (1933). The question must have assumed "such a form that the judicial power is capable of acting on it," *In re Summers, supra* at 567; *Osborn* v. *Bank,* 22 U.S. (9 Wheat.) 738, 819 (1824), and be more than a "desire for an abstract declaration of the law." *In re Summers, supra* at 567; *Fairchild* v. *Hughes,* 258 U.S. 126, 129 (1922); *Muskrat* v. *United States,* 219 U.S. 346, 361 (1911). Although the proceedings in *Summers* were informal and had not been treated as judicial by the Illinois Supreme Court, that court had considered the petition on its merits and rejected it. The Supreme Court of the United States found this treatment had developed the issue sufficiently to make the proceeding adversary.

In the instant case we have exactly the opposite set of circumstances. When Ktsanes petitioned the Illinois court, the petition was merely one for exemption from the rule, not a challenge of it. There was no "claim of a present

---

5. Article III, § 2, Cl. 1 of the Constitution reads:

The judicial Power shall extend to all Cases, in Law an Equity, arising under this Constitution, the Laws of the United States, and Treaties made, or which shall be made, under their Authority;—to all Cases affecting Ambassadors, other public Ministers and Consuls;—to all Cases of admiralty and maritime Jurisdiction;—to Controversies to which the United States shall be a Party;—to Controversies between two or more States;—between a State and Citizens of another State;—between Citizens of different States;—between Citizens of the same State claiming Lands under grants of different States, and between a State, or the Citizens thereof, and foreign States, Citizens or Subjects.

right to admission to the bar of a state and a denial of that right" which the *Summers* Court held to create a case or controversy under Article III. *Summers, supra* at 568. Ktsanes never argued the question of the validity of Rule 705(d) before the Illinois Supreme Court. He was asking for ministerial action, not judicial determination. The denial of his petition was made by the court acting in an administrative capacity. *See Law Students Research Council v. Wadmond,* 401 U.S. 154, 158 n. 9 (1971); *Lathrops v. Donohue,* 367 U.S. 820, 827 (1961). That denial did not present a case or controversy cognizable by an Article III court, and, thus, was not appealable to the Supreme Court of the United States.

The constitutional questions raised by this case were first asserted in the district court; the equal protection issue had nowhere before been litigated. The cases cited by the Attorney General for the proposition that determinations of state courts are appealable only to the United States Supreme Court are inapposite here. *In re Summers, supra; Cromwell v. County of Sac,* 94 U.S. 351 (1876); *Cheramie v. Tucker,* 492 F. 2d 586 (5th Cir. 1974). Those cases involve instances in which the issues were fully developed or in which adversary proceedings had been held. Unlike the instant case, they were appealable to the Supreme Court because they presented cases or controversies within the meaning of Article III.

Defendants present several cases to support their contention that a lower federal court can not hear a challenge to the denial of admission to a state bar. *Doe v. Pringle,* No. 75-1875 (10th Cir., Sept. 24, 1976); *Feldman v. State Board of Law Examiners,* 438 F. 2d 699 (8th Cir. 1971); *MacKay v. Nesbilt,* 412 F. 2d 699 (9th Cir. 1969); *Jones v. Hulse,* 391 F. 2d 198 (8th Cir. 1968). They point to the language in these cases which states, in effect, that admission, discipline, and disbarment of members of a state bar are matters for the state courts, and that federal district courts do not sit as courts on appeal on such matters. This language is generally true; however, the Supreme Court commented in *Schware v. Board of Bar Examiners of the State of New Mexico*, 353 U.S. 232 (1957):

> Admission to practice in a State and before its courts necessarily belongs to that State. Of course, legislation laying down general conditions of an arbitrary or discriminatory character may, like other legislation, fall afoul of the Fourteenth Amendment. 353 U.S. at 248.

This is just such a case, in which the rule "laying down general conditions" is claimed to be discriminatory.

II

Since jurisdiction did exist in the federal district court, we must next determine whether a three-judge court is necessary to hear the case. Defendants argue that no substantial federal question is raised by plaintiff's constitutional challenge to Rule 705(d). The Supreme Court has held that in order to defeat a motion for a three-judge court on this ground, the constitutional attack must be "insubstantial," *Goosby v. Osser*, 409 U.S. 512, 518 (1973), and that this equates with "essentially fictitious," *Bailey v. Patterson*, 369 U.S. 31, 33 (1962), "obviously frivolous," *Hannis Distilling Co. v. Baltimore*, 216 U.S. 285, 288 (1910), or "obviously without merit," *Ex parte Poresky*, 290 U.S. 30, 32 (1933). Thus, in effect, a claim is insubstantial "only if the prior decisions inescapably render the claims frivolous," and not merely doubtful. *Goosby v. Osser, supra* at 518.

There appears to be no Supreme Court case or cases from this circuit which would obviously control the result in this appeal. Defendants' argument on this issue is two-fold: (1) the Supreme Court has decided that different classes of individuals may be treated differently, and this case involves such classes; and (2) this is merely a case of "incidental individual inequality," the kind of case which the Court has held to be not a violation of equal protection.

In addressing defendants' first contention, we note that this is indeed a case involving two different classes. To observe this, however, is not the answer. What is important when a classification is challenged on equal protection grounds is whether there is a rational connection between that classification and some legitimate state interest. This determination goes to the very merits of the claim, and we have not found any controlling decision so as to be able to say that the claim is obviously frivolous. The only case which appears to be on point is *Application of Brewer*, 430 P. 2d 150 (Alas. 1967). That state case does not control this court on the issue of whether a substantial federal question has been raised however persuasive it may be in the final outcome.

We also find defendants' second contention to be without merit. This matter cannot be characterized as one of merely "incidental individual inequality." That phrase is taken from the case of *Phelps* v. *Board of Education*, 300 U.S. 319 (1937), and has been explained by this court to mean that "the question of whether a classification passes constitutional muster cannot be answered by assessing its chance effect upon a particular individual." *Whitfield* v. *Illinois Board of Law Examiners*, 504 F. 2d 474, 476 (7th Cir. 1974). In *Whitfield* the plaintiff claimed that the Illinois bar examination had no connection with an applicant's fitness or capacity to practice law. His claim was based on the fact that he had failed to pass the bar examination after taking it five times, although he alleged his background demonstrated his capability to practice. This court assumed *arguendo* that his background so demonstrated, but found that it was a case of incidental individual inequality, and that the bar examination, in general, was rationally connected to an applicant's capabilities.

The instant case is distinguishable. Plaintiff disputes any rational connection between the fact that one has previously failed the Illinois examination and that person's ability to practice law in Illinois when that person meets the same criteria as an attorney who may be admitted on a foreign license but who has never taken the examination. His claim is not based on the fact that the challenged classification works an inequality in his individual case. Rather, he challenges the rationality of the connection between that classification and the state interest it purportedly serves. We cannot decide whether plaintiff's situation is merely an isolated case of inequality without passing on the merits of his claim. Consequently, that question is reserved for the trial court upon a full consideration of the issue.

We conclude that a substantial federal question exists and that a three-judge court should be convened to hear this matter.

The decision of the district court is reversed.

A true Copy:

     Teste:

                . . . .

                Clerk of the United States Court of
                  Appeals for the Seventh Circuit

APPENDIX B

IN THE

UNITED STATES COURT OF APPEALS
FOR THE SEVENTH CIRCUIT

No. 76-1623

BASIL D. KTSANES,

Plaintiff-Appellant,

v.

HONORABLE ROBERT C. UNDERWOOD, et al.,

Defendants-Appellees.

Appeal from the United States District Court for the Northern District of Illinois, Eastern Division. No. 75-C-3421—Joseph Sam Perry, Judge.

On Petition for Rehearing.

August 15, 1977

PER CURIAM. The petition for rehearing filed by the Attorney General of the State of Illinois on behalf of the defendants-appellees interprets the court's opinion, which is published at 552 F. 2d 740, in a manner not intended. So as to correct any misunderstanding as to the scope of our decision, we believe the following explanation is appropriate.

In his complaint, Ktsanes requested that a three-judge court be convened to hear his constitutional claim. A single district judge may properly dismiss a complaint in which a three-judge court is requested if he concludes that the federal courts lack jurisdiction to hear the case. *Ex Parte Poresky,* 290 U.S. 30 (1933). The district court did hold that it did not have jurisdiction over Ktsanes' complaint. It did so, however, on the grounds that: (1) there is no federal jurisdiction to review a "final decision of the Illinois Supreme Court relating to admission to its bar"; and (2) the Illinois rule did not violate the Equal Protection Clause. This court concluded that the issues which the district court decided, while purportedly jurisdictional, were so bound up with the merits that they should not have been reached by a single judge if the case otherwise met the requirements for the convening of a three-judge district court.

This court then proceeded to determine whether there were any purely jurisdictional bars to federal consideration of the case. In doing so, it decided only two issues. First, it concluded that defendants' denial of plaintiff's request for an exemption from Rule 705(d) of the Supreme Court of Illinois was purely an administrative act and did not qualify as a "case or controversy" under Article III of the Constitution so as to render it directly appealable to the Supreme Court of the United States. Thus, there existed no jurisdictional bar under the doctrines of *res judicata* or collateral estoppel to federal consideration of plaintiff's constitutional claims because plaintiff's action was not a collateral attack upon a *judicial* decision rendered by the Illinois Supreme Court.*

Second, this court decided that the claim presented a substantial federal question sufficient to warrant both federal jurisdiction and the convening of a three-judge district court under 28 U.S.C. § 2281.

Compare Grossgold v. *Supreme Court of Illinois,* —— F. 2d —— (7th Cir. 1977).

Because we concluded that a three-judge court was required, we did not, contrary to the Attorney General's assertion, decide the merits of the case. A three-judge court must still determine: (1) whether on grounds of comity and federalism a federal court is precluded from reviewing the State of Illinois' rejection of an applicant for the Illinois bar, and (2) if not, whether the Illinois rule challenged by Ktsanes violates the Equal Protection Clause. Thus, the scope of the court's decision was far narrower than the State contends.

Accordingly, we reaffirm our previous holding and deny the petition for rehearing.

A true Copy:

Teste:

. . . .
*Clerk of the United States Court of
Appeals for the Seventh Circuit*

UNITED STATES DISTRICT COURT,
NORTHERN DISTRICT OF ILLINOIS
EASTERN DIVISION

Name of Presiding Judge, Honorable Joseph Sam Perry.

Cause No.: 75 C 3421   Date: April 20, 1976

Title of Cause: Basil D. Ktsanes v. Hon. Robert C. Underwood, et al.

This cause comes on upon defendants' motion to dismiss the complaint. The court has read and considered said motion and the memoranda of the respective parties in support thereof and in opposition thereto and finds that said motion should be granted on the grounds that this court lacks jurisdiction to review a final decision of the Illinois Supreme Court relating to admission to its Bar. see *Mac Kay v. Nesbett,* 412 F. 2d 846 (9th Cir. 1969), *cert. denied,* 396 U.S. 960, *reh. denied,* 397 U.S. 1004, and that there is a rational connection between Rule 705(d) of said court and plaintiff's fitness or capacity to practice law in that the rule precludes persons who have taken and failed to pass the Illinois bar examination from using subsequent bar admission in a State with less rigorous requirements as a subterfuge to avoid the more rigorous requirements of the Illinois bar examination. See *Application of Brewer,* 430 P. 2d 150 (Alaska 1967). In the court's view, discussion of other grounds relied upon by the plaintiff is pretermitted.

Accordingly IT IS ORDERED that said motion to dismiss the complaint be and it is hereby granted, and that the complaint herein be and it is hereby DISMISSED with prejudice.

J. S. PERRY.

UNITED STATES COURT OF APPEALS
FOR THE FOURTH CIRCUIT

No. 73-2512

David Richardson, Patricia King ,Patrick Kelly and Hiram Spain, on behalf of themselves and all others similarly situated,

Appellants,

v.

J. Means McFadden, Morris D. Rosen, C. W. F. Spencer, Robert D. Schumpert, David L. Freeman and Albert L. James, Jr., individually and as members of the State Board of Law Examiners: and Miss Frances Smith, Clerk of the Supreme Court of South Carolina,

Appellees.

No. 73-2513

David Richardson, Patricia King, Patrick Kelly and Hiram Spain, on behalf of themselves and all others similarly situated,

Appellees,

v.

J. Means McFadden, Morris D. Rosen, C. W. F. Spencer, Robert D. Schumpert, David L. Freeman and Albert L. James, Jr., individually and as members of the State Board of Law Examiners: and Miss Frances Smith, Clerk of the Supreme Court of South Carolina,

Appellants.

Appeals from the United States District Court for the District of South Carolina, at Charleston. Sol Blatt, Jr., District Judge.

Reargued March 15, 1977   Decided October 12, 1977

Before HAYNSWORTH, Chief Judge, BOREMAN, Senior Circuit Judge, WINTER, CRAVEN,* BUTZNER, RUS-SELL, WIDENER, and HALL, Circuit Judges, sitting in banc on resubmission.

Ray P. McClain and F. Henderson Moore (Laughlin Mc-Donald, Neil Bradley, Melvin L. Wulf, E. Richard Larson on brief) for Appellants in 73-2512 and for Appellees in 73-2513; Randall T. Bell (Daniel R. McLeod, Attorney General of South Carolina and A. Camden Lewis, Assistant Attorney General of South Carolina on brief) for Appellees in 73-2512 and for Appellants in 73-2513.

PER CURIAM:

We granted rehearing in banc to reconsider the issues decided by a panel of the court in Richardson v. McFadden, 540 F. 2d 744 (4 Cir. 1976). There, in an action for declaratory and injunctive relief brought by four black law school graduates who had satisfied all requirements for admission to the South Carolina Bar, except that they received failing scores on the bar examination, the panel decided that the district court properly denied relief except for the individual claims of Spain and Kelly. With respect to them, the panel concluded that the Law Examiners had acted arbitrarily and capriciously, and it directed the district court to order them to be certified as having passed the South Carolina Bar.

---

*Judge Craven died before this opinion was prepared.

I

Except with respect to the individual claims of Spain and Kelly, we see no merit in plaintiffs' various contentions for the reasons assigned by the panel.

II

With regard to the individual claims of Spain and Kelly, we conclude, in disagreement with the panel, that the district court correctly denied relief.

At the outset, we recognize that a jurisdictional question is raised by the assertion of individual claims for relief by Spain and Kelly, i.e., whether, in judging the intellectual fitness of applicants to practice law, the Law Examiners performed a judicial function on behalf of the South Carolina Supreme Court, so that under such precedents as Doe v. Pringle, 550 F. 2d 596 (10 Cir. 1976), *cert. denied*, —— U.S. —— (1977), and McKay v. Nesbett, 412 F. 2d 846 (9 Cir. 1969), *cert. denied*, 396 U.S. 960 (1969), we should conclude that the district court lacked subject matter jurisdiction to review the denial of admission to the bar. We are divided on how this issue should be decided, but we find it unnecessary to debate or resolve our differences because a clear majority of us agrees that, even if the district court had subject matter jurisdiction, the proof will not support the conclusion that Spain and Kelly are entitled to individual relief.

Their claim to relief is founded upon due process and equal protection claims. Before turning to the factual basis of their claims, we stress that our function is not just to determine if the bar examiners made a mistake in one or more individual cases; it is to determine if there has been a denial of due process or of equal protection. Not every erroneous determination mounts up to a denial of due process or equal protection. Bishop v. Wood, 426 U.S. 341, 349-50 (1976).

Factually, Kelly and Spain showed that *other* applicants at *other* times appeared to have received more favorable treatment in grading than that which was afforded them. See table at 540 F. 2d at 750. Specifically, Spain, who was a June, 1971, applicant having an average score of 70.5 and having been failed by three examiners, points to applicant 129, a June, 1970, applicant having an average score of 71.8 and also having been failed by three examiners, who was passed. Kelly, who was a February, 1971, applicant having an average score of 69.6 and having been failed by three examiners, points to applicant 10, also a February, 1971, applicant who was passed with an average score of 69.3 but who was failed by only two examiners.

We do not think this proof establishes the constitutional discrimination requisite to the granting of individual relief. In the case of Spain, the comparison urged on us is of different years. While the mere fact of different years does not make the comparison inapposite, all of the circumstances which make the two instances comparable were not shown. Moreover, the record does not show that in grading Spain the examiners had before them the record of what had been done the year before. In the case of Kelly, the fact that he was failed by three examiners serves to distinguish his case from the asserted analogue where the applicant was failed by only two examiners. The further fact that a February, 1970, applicant (No. 17) was failed with an average of 69.5 after having been failed by only two examiners does not destroy the distinction. Although it occurred in a different examination from the one about which Kelly complains, it may show discrimination with reference to 17; but Kelly can hardly advance his cause as a result of a possible due process violations to another. Significant also, with respect to Spain and Kelly, are the facts that of the aggregate 828 examinations given during the eight times that the bar examination was administered over a four-year period, only these two examples of alleged discrimination were proved, and that Spain and Kelly continued to fail on subsequent reexaminations. Succinctly stated, we simply do not think that Spain and Kelly proved their case.

Since we conclude that there was no error in the judgment of the district court on any of the grounds asserted, its judgment is

AFFIRMED.

HALL, Circuit Judge, concurring in the result:

While I concur in the result reached in this case, I do so because I believe that the district court was without subject matter jurisdiction to review the questions relating to the individual admissions to the bar of Spain and Kelly. Settled precedents, I believe, support my views regarding the district court's lack of subject matter jurisdiction.

In South Carolina, the exclusive jurisdiction to pass upon the qualifications of applicants is vested in the South Carolina Supreme Court by both the state constitution and by statute. S. C. CONST. art. V, § 4; S.C. CODE § 56-96. By administering the bar examination and judging the intellectual fitness of applicants to practice law, the Law Examiners perform a judicial function on behalf of the South Carolina Supreme Court.[1] The South Carolina Su-

1. See Deposition of J. Means McFadden, App. at 428-29:

> Well we [Law Examiners] are subject to the control of the Supreme Court, and we take no action of an affirmative nature without first conferring with the Supreme Court and getting their approval of it. * * * [W]e are subject to their supervision in every thing we do. But to the extent that we have to formulate questions, give the

examination, grade the papers, yes, we have to do that on an individual basis. There is no other way we can do it. [However, before any changes were made in the scheme of the examination], we got the approval of the Supreme Court before we ever put in changes.

preme Court thus exercises judicial power within the scope of its subject matter and personal jurisdiction when it acts upon the admission of applicants to the state bar. And while that court is not required to admit an applicant to the South Carolina Bar simply because the Bar Examiners have certified that he has passed the bar examination,[2] nevertheless the failure to obtain such a certification does preclude admittance to the bar.

Many states have statutorily established a formal procedure for petitioning the states' highest court for review of an adverse determination by a board of bar examiners who failed to certify that an applicant has passed a bar examination. A statutory provision such as this did not exist in South Carolina during the time relevant to this case; however, petitions by aggrieved bar applicants had been made to and considered by the South Carolina Supreme Court.[3] Final action on an application to the state

---

2. However, the record does not reflect any instance when the South Carolina Supreme Court refused to follow the recommendations of its Law Examiners in admitting applicants to the bar.

3. After instituion of this suit, the South Carolina Supreme Court voluntarily did establish by rule procedures for the review of failing papers. *See* Rule 11, RULES FOR THE EXAMINATION AND ADMISSION OF PERSONS TO PRACTICE LAW IN SOUTH CAROLINA (effective date—February 10, 1975).

bar is by the South Carolina Supreme Court, whether the action taken is expressed or implied;[4] and review from an adverse decision is secured by petitioning the Supreme Court of the United States for certiorari. *Schware v. Board of Bar Examiners of New Mexico*, 353 U.S. 232 (1957); *Konigsberg v. State Bar of California*, 353 U.S. 252 (1957); *Theard v. United States*, 354 U.S. 278 (1957). Three circuits are in accord. *See Doe v. Pringle*, 550 F. 2d 596 (10th Cir. 1976), *cert. denied,* —— U.S. ——, 97 S. Ct. 2179 (1977); *Feldman v. State Board of Law Examiners,* 438 F. 2d 699 (8th Cir. 1971); *MacKay v. Nesbett*, 412 F. 2d 846 (9th Cir. 1969), *cert. denied,* 396 U.S. 960 (1969); *Gately v. Sutton,* 310 F. 2d 107 (10th Cir. 1962).

The United States Court of Appeals for the Tenth Circuit has recently considered this particular jurisdictional issue in *Doe v. Pringle, supra*. There, a frustrated bar ap-

---

4. *See American Civil Liberties Union v. Bozardt,* 539 F. 2d 340 (4th Cir. 1976), *cert. denied,* 97 S. Ct. 639 (1976). where a final (appealable) state adjudication of a disciplinary proceeding was said not to occur until it could be demonstrated that the South Carolina Supreme Court either expressly decided the question or *acquiesced* in the decision of the Board of Commissioners on Grievances and Discipline of the South Carolina Bar.

The fictitious *"Jane Koe"* in *Bozardt*, in reality Ms. Edna Smith, subsequently did seek a direct review of the private reprimand administered by the Board of Commissioners on Grievances and Discipline. The Supreme Court of South Carolina reviewed the case but ordered a public reprimand. *Matter of Smith*, 233 S.E. 2d 301, 306 (S.C. 1977).

An appeal to the Supreme Court of the United States was then filed. *In Re Smith*, No. 77-56; 46 U.S.L.W. 3041. It is currently pending.

plicant had brought a civil rights action challenging the state supreme court's denial of his aplication for admission to the bar, despite a favorable recommendation of the bar committee. Upholding the district court's dismissal of the action, the Tenth Circuit ruled that a federal court was without subject matter jurisdiction to review the denial of admission to the bar even though plaintiffs' challenge was anchored to an alleged deprivation of federally protected due process and equal protection rights.

Drawing from the district court's ruling, the *Doe* court noted that there is a subtle but fundamental distinction between two types of claims which a disappointed bar applicant might bring to federal court:

> The first is a constitutional challenge to the state's general rules and regulations governing admission; the second is a claim based on constitutional or other grounds, that the state has unlawfully denied a particular applicant admission.

Doe, 550 F. 2d at 597.

Thus,

> [W]hile federal courts do exercise jurisdiction over many constitutional claims which atack the state's power to license atorneys involving challenges to either the rule-making authority or the administration of the rules [citations omitted], *such is not true where review of a state court's jurisdiction of a particular application is sought.* * * * [T]he latter claim may be heard, if at all, exclusively by the Supreme Court of the United States. . . . [relying on the 'Theard Doctrine' announced in *Theard* v. *United States,* 354 U.S. 278 (1957)].

Doe, 550 F. 2d at 597.

The Eighth Circuit, in *Feldman* v. *State Board of Law Examiners,* 438 F. 2d 699 (8th Cir. 1971) dealt with a plaintiff who had twice failed the Arkansas bar exam, who sued the Board, and others, seeking injunctive relief and based jurisdiction upon 28 U.S.C. §§ 1343(3) and 1331(a). He sought to state a claim under 42 U.S.C. § 1983. The district court initially expressed doubt as to its subject matter jurisdiction but, dismissed on nonjurisdictional grounds. The Court of Apeals noted that the suit proerly could have been dismissed on jurisdictional grounds, 438 F. 2d at 701, and then noted that:

> ". . . plaintiff's remedy if any lies in presenting his grievance to the Arkansas Supreme Court. If the ruling these is adverse to him, he may aply for certiorari to the United States Supreme Court in the manner as was done in *Schware, Konigsberg* and *Theard.* As the trial court proerly stated, it is not an apellate court and cannot in such a case as this review State court actions."

Feldman, 438 F. 2d at 704.

Finally, in *MacKay* v. *Nesbett,* supra, the Ninth Circuit was faced with a challenge to the action of a majority of the Justices of the Alaska Supreme Court who had entered disciplinary orders suspending MacKay from the practice of law for a period of one year. Relying upon *Theard* and *Gately,* supra, and other precedent in suport of the *Theard* doctrine, the court said:

> [O]rders of a state court relating to the *admission,* discipline, and disbarment of members of its bar may be reviewed only by the Supreme Court of the United States on certiorari to the state court and not by means of an original action in the lower federal court. The rule serves substantial policy interests arising from the historic relationship between state judicial systems and the members of their respective bars, and between the state and federal judicial systems.

MacKay, 412 F. 2d at 846. Emphasis added.

While we are aware that there is some authority to the contrary in the Seventh and perhas the Fifth Circuits,[5] and while we are fully appreciative of the desirable goal of avoidin, if possible, the creation of a conflict among our sister circuits, I nevertheless believe we should follow the teachings of *Doe, Feldman* and *MacKay,* and accordingly, I would hold that the district court should have dismissed the claims of Spain and Kelly regarding their allegations of having been wrongfully deprived of passing grades on the South Carolina Bar Examination. By failing to admit Spain and Kelly to the South Carolina Bar, the South Carolina Supreme Court had acquiesced in the Board of Law Examiners' recommendation to not license them. Review of this denial lies exclusively with the Supreme Court of the United States.

Judge Widener authorizes me to state that he joins in this opinion.

BOREMAN, Senior Circuit Judge, concurring specially in the result:

As a Senior Circuit Judge I was a member of the panel of three which considered and decided the apeal. Having served on that panel I was qualified to participate in the rehearing in banc which was ordered by the court.

---

5. *See Whitfield v. Illinois Board of Law Examiners,* 504 F. 2d 474, 477 (7th Cir. 1974):

Plaintiff, of course, did allege that defendants acted arbitrarily in grading his examination. There may very well be situations in which a capricious denial by state officials may give rise to a federal remedy. (dictum).

See also Tyler v. Vickery, 517 F. 2d 1089 (5th Cir. 1975), *cert. denied,* 426 U.S. 940 (1976).

Upon the rehearing in banc I have ben persuaded that the jurisdictional question raised was not accorded the serious consideration by the panel to which it was entitled. From the arguments presented, in briefs and orally, and upon careful review of the opinions of other highly respected circuit courts of appeals I am convinced that the federal district court should have dismissed this action for lack of subject matter jurisdiction.

Therefore, I join Judge Hall in his opinon in which he concurs in the result and for the reasons as set forth by him therein.

No. 77-691

2-14-78

In the
Supreme Court of the United States

OCTOBER TERM, 1977

SUPREME COURT OF ILLINOIS,
HONORABLE DANIEL P. WARD, et al.,

Petitioners,

vs.

BASIL D. KTSANES,

Respondent.

RESPONDENT'S BRIEF IN OPPOSITION TO PETITION FOR WRIT OF CERTIORARI TO THE UNITED STATES COURT OF APPEALS FOR THE SEVENTH CIRCUIT

JASON E. BELLOWS
One IBM Plaza
Suite 1414
Chicago, Illinois 60611
Attorney for Respondent

UNITED STATES LAW PRINTING CO., CHICAGO, ILLINOIS 60618   (312) 525-6581

INDEX

In the
Supreme Court of the United States

OCTOBER TERM, 1977

No. 77-691

SUPREME COURT OF ILLINOIS,
HONORABLE DANIEL P. WARD, et al.,

Petitioners,

vs.

BASIL D. KTSANES,

Respondent.

RESPONDENT'S BRIEF IN OPPOSITION TO PETITION FOR WRIT OF CERTIORARI TO THE UNITED STATES COURT OF APPEALS FOR THE SEVENTH CIRCUIT

QUESTION PRESENTED

Whether a petition to the Illinois Supreme Court requesting a waiver of a provision of one of its rules is a case or controversy within the meaning of Article III of the Constitution of the United States.

STATEMENT

This case was commenced by a complaint in the United States District Court for the Northern District of Illinois, seeking declaratory relief and an injunction against the Petitioners here restraining them from enforcing the provisions of Rule 705(d) of the Rules of the Supreme Court of Illinois. That rule provides that an attorney cannot be admitted to practice in Illinois on a foreign license, even though he/she has met all of the other requirements for admission on a foreign license, if that attorney has previously taken the Illinois Bar examination and failed it. Prior to this proceeding the Respondent here petitioned the Supreme Court of Illinois to waive that provision of its rules. The petition was denied. Thereafter, the Respondent directly attacked the rule in the United States District Court by this proceeding. At no time before the Illinois Supreme Court, did the Respondent make any attempt to litigate the question presented to the Court.

ARGUMENT

The case, as decided by the United States Court of Appeals, turned on a narrow question to which the Petitioners here have completely failed to address themselves. That question is whether the original petition to Supreme Court of Illinois for a waiver of its rules was a case or controversy within the meaning of Article III of the Constitution of the United States. The Court of Appeals for the Seventh Circuit determined that that petition was not a case or controversy and therefore the Supreme Court of the United States could not have reviewed the question of the correctness of the decision of the Illinois Supreme Court, and the Court of Appeals further concluded that this attack on the rule of Court does not constitute a review of any decision made by the Supreme Court of Illinois in its judicial capacity.

As the Court of Appeals recognized in its petition the case is controlled by the decision of this Court *In Re Summers*, 325 U.S. 561.

In *Summers*, the Petitioner had attempted to gain admission to the Illinois Bar and was denied admission because of his conscientious objection to taking an oath to support the Constitution of Illinois.

The case there arose out of the refusal of the Committee on Character and Fitness, appointed by the Supreme Court of Illinois, to certify the good character of the Petitioner Summers. Summers then petitioned to the Supreme Court of Illinois attacking this refusal of the Committee on Character and Fitness and the Supreme Court of Illinois denied Summers petition to be admitted notwithstanding the unfavorable report of the Committee on Character and Fitness. It was from that decision of the Supreme Court of Illinois that Summers sought review in this Court.

The justices of the Supreme Court of Illinois contended that there was no case or controversy within the meaning of the provisions of Article III of the Constitution of the United States. In rejecting that contention this Court stated:

> A case arises within the meaning of the Constitution when any question respecting the Constitution, treatise or laws of the United States has assumed "such a form that the judicial power is capable of acting on it." *Osborne* v. *Bank*, 9 Wheat. 738, 819.

> The Court was then considering the power of the Bank to sue in the Federal court. The declaration on rights as they stand must be sought not on rights which may arise in the future, *Prentice* v. *Atlantic Coast Line Company, Co.*, 211 U.S. 210, 226, and there must be an actual controversy over an issue, not a desire for an abstract declaration of law. *Muskrat* v. *United States*, 219 U.S. 346, 361; *Fairchild* v. *Hughes*, 228 U.S. 126, 129. The form of the proceeding is not significant. It is the nature and effect which is controlling. *Nashville, C. & St. L. Ry.* v. *Wallace*, 288 U.S. 249. (325 U.S. at pp. 566, 567.)

Later, the Court added:

> "A claim of a present right to admission to the bar of a State and a denial of that right is a controversy. When the claim is made in a State court and a denial of the right is made by a judicial order, it is a case which may be reviewed under Article III of the Constitution when Federal questions are raised and proper steps taken to that end in this Court." (325 U.S. at pp. 568, 569.)

The Court of Appeals in this case, in its opinion, concluded:

> In the instant case we have exactly the opposite set of circumstances. When Ktsanes petitioned the Illinois court, the petition was merely one for exemption from the rule, not a challenge of it. There was no

'claim of a present right to admission to a bar of a State and a denial of that right' which the *Summers* court held to create a case or controversy under Article III. *Summers, supra.* at 568. Ktsanes never argued the question of the validity of Rule 705(d) before the Illinois Supreme Court. He was asking for ministerial action, not judicial determination. The denial of his petition was made by the Court acting in an administrative capacity. See, *Law Students Research Counsel v. Wadmond,* 401 U.S. 154, 158 n.9 (1971); Lathrop v. Donohue, 367 U.S. 820, 827 (1961). That denial did not present a case or controversy cognizable by an Article III court and, thus, was not appealable to the Supreme Court of the United States.

A case of similar import is *Lathrop v. Donohue,* 367 U.S. 820 (1961) in which the Supreme Court of Wisconsin entered an order integrating the Bar of Wisconsin. The question before the Supreme Court of the United States was whether the order was a statute for the purposes of 28 U.S.C. § 1257(2). In *Lathrop* the Court, although divided on the question of whether Wisconsin could compel an attorney to pay dues to an organization taking positions to which he was opposed, recognized the legislative characteristics of the order and the lack of its judicial quality.

Here the Supreme Court of Illinois exercising its inherent power to regulate the practice of law has adopted a series of rules for admission to the Bar. The refusal of the Illinois Court to waive its rule in this regard was not a judicial act after a hearing or adversary proceeding.

Perhaps the leading case on the question of the jurisdiction of a Federal Court in a case such as this is *Law Students Civil Rights Research Council, Inc. v. Wadmond,* (S.D.N.Y. 1969), 299 F. Supp. 117. In that case certain law students and others attempted to have struck down certain requirements and procedures for admission to the bar of the State of New York. The defendants were two of the Appellate Divisions of the Supreme Court of the State of New York, the Committees on Character and Fitness of the two divisions of the Supreme Court, and the justices and the members thereof. The question of jurisdiction was presented and Judge Friendly, speaking for the Court, stated as follows:

> We fail to perceive what interest would be served by holding Federal courts to be powerless to enjoin state officers from acting under a statute that allegedly deprives citizens of rights protected by the Civil Rights Act or promulgating regulations that are alleged to have that result simply because some of them are robed and others have been appointed by those who are. Rather it would seem anomalous that while Federal courts could entertain a complaint similar to the plaintiffs if made with respect to other licensed professions, such as medicine or accountability, they are powerless with respect to admission to the bar. The grant of injunctive relief in a case like this would not have in terrorem effect on state judges that the threat of a subsequent damage action would have; rather, it would furnish a definitive ruling on a point of Federal law for their future guidance, and, would not infringe the policy expressed in the Federal anti-injunction statute, 28 U.S.C. §2283, proscribing injunctions that would stay court "proceedings in a State court."

In the above-cited case, the District court of three judges granted only a small portion of the relief sought and an appeal was taken pursuant 28 U.S.C. §1253, directly to this Court. This court, in *Law Students Civil Rights Research Council, Inc.* v. *Wadmond*, 401 U.S. 154, 91 S.Ct. 720, perfunctorily affirmed the jurisdiction of the District Court. 401 U.S. 154, 158, N. 9.

A case containing similar facts in some respects to the present case is *Keenan* v. *Board of Law Examiners of the State of North Carolina* (E.D.N.C. 1970) 317 F. Supp. 1350, in which certain persons made application for an admission to the bar of North Carolina and said applications were not acted upon because the applicants had not met the North Carolina residency requirement.

The three-judge district court in *Keenan* disposed of the contention that the plaintiffs there were in effect seeking review of a matter that came within the peculiar competence of the North Carolina courts by stating as follows:

> "These plaintiffs do not challenge a state court's disposition of an individual case; their personal circumstances merely furnish concreteness to a class action attacking a general rule as facially unconstitutional. Their assertion that they have been excluded from the practice of their profession in violation of the equal protection clause of the 14th Amendment is sufficient to allege a claim for relief under the Civil Rights Act, 42 U.S.C. §1983, and under 28 U.S.C. §1343(3). The right not to be so excluded is secured to them by the Constitution. Schware v. Board of Bar Examiners [353 U.S. 232, 77 S.Ct. 752 (1957)]. We therefore reject the Board's challenge to our jurisdiction over the subject matter of this case."

The court in *Keenan* also referred to Mr. Justice Frankfurter's concurrent opinion in *Schware* in which he defined the distinction between the review of the individual case and the review of general conditions for admission as follows:

> "Admission to practice in a state and before its courts necessarily belongs to the State. Of course, legislation laying down general conditions of an arbitrary or discriminatory character may, like other legislation, fall afoul of the 14th Amendment * * * A very different question is presented when this court is asked to review the exercise of judgment in refusing admission to the bar in an individual case, such as we have here. It is beyond this court's function to act as overseer of a particular result of a procedure established by a particular state for admission to its bar." 353 U.S. at 248, 77 S.Ct. at 761.

It is clear from the record in this case that no exercise of judgment was involved in the refusal of the defendants bar examiners or justices of the Supreme Court to admit the plaintiff on a foreign license. They were merely administering the rules of court pertaining to the admission to the bar as they were promulgated by the Supreme Court of Illinois. It is those rules rather than any specific action in a specific case that are being questioned here.

The Petitioners contend that principles of comity require that the federal courts abstain from action in this case. None of the cases relied upon by the Petitioners may be so construed.

Judice v. *Vail*, ... U.S. ...., 97 S. Ct. 1211, clearly limits its doctrine to pending cases. As the Court said, quoting from *Ex Parte Young*, 209 U.S. 123 (1908):

> But the Federal court cannot, of course, interfere in a case where the proceedings were already pending in a state court. * * * 209 U.S., at 162.

The operative word here is "case" and "pending." As the Court of Appeals correctly held, there was no "case" and therefore the Federal Courts are not interfering in a State case much less a pending state case.

As we have stated above this case is merely an attempt to have a rule of the Supreme Court of Illinois declared unconstitutional. The question presented is neither insubstantial nor frivolous, and the Court of Appeals was correct in ordering the convening of a Three Judge District Court.

Conclusion

For the above and foregoing reasons, the petition for a writ of certiorari ought to be denied.

Respectfully submitted,

JASON E. BELLOWS
Attorney for respondent

CPSIA information can be obtained
at www.ICGtesting.com
Printed in the USA
LVHW060823060323
741015LV00012BA/475